NO TRIFLING WITH LOVE
A COMEDY IN THREE ACTS

BY

ALFRED DE MUSSET

(PUBLISHED IN 1834; ACTED IN 1861)

DONE INTO ENGLISH BY
M. RAOUL PELLISSIER

(1905.)

Edited by
B. K. De Fabris

TIMELESS📖CLASSICS

CHARACTERS

THE BARON.
PERDICAN, *His Son.*
MASTER BLAZIUS, *Perdican's Tutor.*
MASTER BRIDAINE, *Parish Priest.*
CAMILLE, *the Baron's Niece.*
DAME PLUCHE, *Her Governess.*
ROSETTEETTE, *Foster-sister of Camille.*
Peasants, Servants, etc.

ACT THE FIRST

SCENE I

(A village green before the château.)

CHORUS. Gently rocked on his prancing mule, Master Blazius advances through the blossoming corn-flowers; his clothes are new, his writing-case hangs by his side. Like a chubby baby on a pillow, he rolls about on top of his protuberant belly, and with his eyes half closed mumbles a paternoster into his double chin. Welcome, Master Blazius; you come for the vintage-time in the semblance of an ancient amphora.

BLAZIUS. Let those who wish to learn an important piece of news first of all bring me here a glass of new wine.

CHORUS. Here is our biggest bowl: drink, Master Blazius; the wine is good; you shall speak afterward.

BLAZIUS. You are to know, my children, that young Perdican, our signor's son, has just attained his majority, and that he has taken his doctor's degree at Paris. This very day he comes home to the château with his mouth full of such fine flowery phrases, that three-quarters of the time you do not know how to answer him. His charming person is just all one golden book; he can not see a blade of grass on the ground without giving you the Latin name for it; and when it blows or when it rains he tells you plainly the reason why. You will open your eyes as wide as the gate there to see him unroll one of the scrolls he has illuminated in ink of all colors, all with his own hands, and not a word said to anybody. In short, he is a polished diamond from top to toe, and that is the message I am bringing to my lord the Baron. You perceive that does some credit to me, who have been his tutor since he was four years old; so now, my good friends, bring a chair and let me just get off this mule without breaking my neck; the beast is a trifle restive, and I should not be sorry to drink another drop before going in.

CHORUS. Drink, Master Blazius, and recover your wits. We saw little Perdican born, and once you said, he is coming, we did not need to hear such a long story about him. May we find the child in the grown man's heart!

BLAZIUS. On my word the bowl is empty; I did not think I had drunk it all. Good-by! As I trotted along the road I got ready two or three unpretending phrases that will please my lord; I will go and pull the bell. *(Exit.)*

CHORUS. Sorely jolted on her panting ass, Dame Pluche mounts the hill. Her frightened groom belabors the poor animal with all his might, while it shakes its head with a thistle in its jaws. Her long lean legs jerk with anger, whilst her bony hands string off her beads. Good-day to you, Dame Pluche; you come like the fever with the wind that colors the leaves.

PLUCHE. A glass of water, you rabble; a glass of water and a little vinegar.

CHORUS. Where do you come from, Pluche, my darling? Your false hair is covered with dust; there's a wig spoiled; and your chaste gown is tucked up to your venerable garters.

PLUCHE. Know, boors, that the fair Camilla, your master's niece, arrives at the château to-day. She left the convent by my lord's express orders to come and enter on possession of her mother's rich estate, in due time and place, as much is to be done. Her education, thank God, is finished, and those who see her will have the fortune to inhale the fragrance of a glorious flower of goodness and piety. Never was there anything so pure, so lamb-like, so dovelike, as that dear novice; the Lord God of heaven be her guide: Amen. Stand aside, you rabble; I fancy my legs are swollen.

CHORUS. Smooth yourself down, honest Pluche, and when you pray to God ask for rain; our corn is as dry as your shanks.

PLUCHE. You have brought me water in a bowl that smells of the kitchen. Give me a hand to help me down. You are a pack of ill-mannered boobies. *(Exit.)*

CHORUS. Let us put on our Sunday best, and wait till the Baron sends for us. Either I am greatly mistaken, or there is to be some jolly merry-making to-day.

SCENE II

(The Barons drawing-room. Enter the Baron, Master Bridaine, and Master Blazius.)

BARON. Master Bridaine, you are my friend: let me introduce Master Blazius, my son's tutor. My son yesterday, at eight minutes past twelve, noon, was exactly twenty-one years old. He has taken his degree, and passed in four subjects. Master Blazius, I introduce to you Master Bridaine, priest of the parish, and my friend.

BLAZIUS. *(bowing)*. Passed in four subjects, your lordship: literature, philosophy, Roman law, canon law.

BARON. Go to your room, my dear Blazius; my son will not be long in appearing. Arrange your dress a little, and return when the bell rings.

(Exit Master Blazius.)

BRIDAINE. Shall I tell you what I am thinking, my lord? Your son's tutor smells strongly of wine.

BARON. It is impossible!

BRIDAINE. I am as sure as I am alive. He spoke to me very closely just now. He smells terribly of wine.

BARON. No more of this. I repeat, it is impossible.

(Enter Dame Pluche.)

BARON. There you are, good Dame Pluche! My niece is with you, no doubt?

PLUCHE. She is following me, my lord. I preceded her by a few steps.

BARON. Master Bridaine, you are my friend. I present to you Dame Pluche, my niece's governess. My niece, yesterday at seven o'clock P.M., attained the age of eighteen years. She is leaving the best convent in France. Dame Pluche, I present to you Master Bridaine, priest of the parish, and my friend.

PLUCHE *(bowing)*. The best convent in France, my lord; and, I may add, the best Christian in the convent.

BARON. Go, Dame Pluche, and repair the disorder you are in. My niece will be here shortly, I hope. Be ready at the dinner-hour.

(Exit Dame Pluche.)

BRIDAINE. That old lady seems full of unction.

BARON. Full of unction and compunction, Master Bridaine. Her virtue is unassailable.

BRIDAINE. But the tutor smells of wine. I am absolutely certain of it.

BARON. Master Bridaine, there are moments when I doubt your friendship. Are you setting yourself to contradict me? Not a word more on that matter. I have formed the project of marrying my son to my niece. They are a couple made for one another. Their education has stood me in six thousand crowns.

BRIDAINE. It will be necessary to obtain a dispensation.

BARON. I have it, Bridaine; it is in my study on the table. Oh, my friend, let me tell you now that I am full of joy. You know I have always detested solitude. Nevertheless, the position I occupy and the seriousness of my character compel me to reside in this château for three months every summer and winter. It is impossible to insure the happiness of men in general, and one's vassals in particular, without sometimes giving one's valet the stern order to admit no one. How austere and irksome is the statesman's retirement! and what pleasure may I not hope to find in mitigating, by the presence of my wedded children, the melancholy gloom to which I have been inevitably a prey since the King saw fit to appoint me collector!

BRIDAINE. Will the marriage be performed here or at Paris?

BARON. That is just what I expected, Bridaine. I was certain you would ask that. Well, then, my friend—what would you say if those very hands—yes, Bridaine, your own hands—do not look at them so deprecatingly—were destined solemnly to bless the happy realization of my dearest dreams? Eh?

BRIDAINE. I am silent; gratitude seals my lips.

BARON. Look out of this window; do you not see my servants crowding to the gate? My two children are arriving at the same moment: it is the happiest combination. I have arranged things in such a way that all is foreseen; my niece will be introduced by this door on the left, my son by the door on the right. What do you say to that? It will be the greatest delight to me to see how they will address one another, and what they will say. Six thousand crowns is no trifle, there's no mistake about that. Besides, the children loved each other tenderly from the cradle. Bridaine, I have an idea—

BRIDAINE. What?

BARON. During dinner, without seeming to mean anything by it—you understand, my friend? —while emptying some merry glass——you know Latin, Bridaine?

BRIDAINE. *Ita œdepol*, by Jove, I should think so.

BARON. I should be very pleased to see you put the lad through his paces—discreetly of course—before his cousin: that can not fail to produce a good effect. Make him speak a little Latin; not exactly during dinner, that would spoil our appetites, and as for me, I do not understand a word of it: but at dessert, do you see?

BRIDAINE. If you do not understand a word of it, my lord, probably your niece is in the same plight.

BARON. All the more reason. Would you have a woman admire what she understands? Where were you brought up, Bridaine? That is a lamentable piece of reasoning.

BRIDAINE. I do not know much about women; but it seems to me difficult to admire what one does not understand.

BARON. Ah, Bridaine, I know them; I know the charming indefinable creatures! Be convinced that they love to have dust in their eyes, and the faster one throws, the wider they strain them to catch more.

(Enter on one side Perdican, Camille on the other.)

BARON. Good day, children; good day, my dear Camille, and you, my dear Perdican: kiss me and kiss each other.

PERDICAN. Good day, father, and you, my darling cousin. How delightful; how happy I am!

CAMILLE. How do you do, uncle? and you, cousin?

PERDICAN. How tall you are, Camille, and beautiful as the day!

BARON. When did you leave Paris, Perdican?

PERDICAN. Wednesday, I think—or Tuesday. Why, you are transformed into a woman! So I am a man, am I? It seems only yesterday I saw you only so high.

BARON. You must both be tired; it is a long journey, and the day is hot.

PERDICAN. Oh, dear, no! Look how pretty Camille is, father.

BARON. Come, Camille, give your cousin a kiss.

CAMILLE. Pardon me.

BARON. A compliment is worth a kiss. Give her a kiss, Perdican.

PERDICAN. If my cousin draws back when I hold out my hand, I will say to you in my turn: pardon me. Love may steal a kiss, friendship never.

CAMILLE. Neither friendship nor love should accept anything but what they can give back.

BARON *(to Master Bridaine).* This is an ill-omened beginning, eh?

BRIDAINE. *(to the Baron).* Too much modesty is a fault, no doubt; but marriage does away with a deal of scruples.

BARON *(to Master Bridaine).* I am shocked—I am hurt. That answer displeased me. Pardon me! Did you see that she made a show of crossing herself? Come here, and let me speak to you. It pains me to the last degree. This moment, that was to be so sweet, is wholly spoiled for me. I am vexed, annoyed. The devil take it; it is a regular bad business.

BRIDAINE. Say a few words to them; look at them turning their backs on each other.

BARON. Well, children, what in the world are you thinking of? What are you doing there, Camille, in front of that tapestry?

CAMILLE. *(looking at a picture).* That is a fine portrait, uncle. Is it not a great-aunt of ours?

BARON. Yes, my child, it is your great-grandmother—or, at least, your great-grandfather's sister; for the dear lady never contributed —except, I believe, in prayers—to the augmentation of the family. She was a pious woman, upon my honor.

CAMILLE. Oh, yes, a saint. She is my great-aunt Isabel. How that nun's dress becomes her!

BARON. And you, Perdican, what are you about before that flower-pot?

PERDICAN. That's a charming flower, father. It is a heliotrope.

BARON. Are you joking? It is no bigger than a fly.

PERDICAN. That little flower no bigger than a fly is worth having all the same.

BRIDAINE. No doubt the doctor is right. Ask him what sex or what class it belongs to, of what elements it consists, whence it gets its sap and its color: he will throw you into ecstasies with a description of the phenomena of yonder sprig, from its root to its flower.

PERDICAN. I do not know so much about it, your reverence. I think it smells good, that is all.

SCENE III

(Before the château. Enter the Chorus.)

CHORUS. Several things amuse us and excite our curiosity. Come, friends, sit down under this walnut tree. Two formidable eaters are this moment present at the château—Master Bridaine and Master Blazius. Have you not noticed this—that when two men, closely alike, equally fat and fond of drink, with the same vices and the same passions, come to a meeting by some chance, it follows of necessity that they shall either adore or abominate each other? For the same reason that opposites attract, that a tall lean man will like a short round one, that fair people court the dark, and *vice versa*, I foresee a secret struggle between the tutor and the priest. Both are armed with equal impudence, each has a barrel for a belly; they are not only gluttons, but epicures; both will quarrel at table for quality as well as quantity. If the fish is small, what is to be done? And in any case a carp's tongue can not be divided, and a carp can not have two tongues... Then both are chatterers; but if the worst should come to the worst, they can talk at once and neither listen to the other. Already Master Bridaine has wanted to put several pedantic questions to young Perdican, and the tutor scowled. It is distasteful to him that his pupil should appear to be examined by any one but himself. Again, one is as ignorant as the other. Again, they are priests, the pair of them: one will parade his benefice, the other will plume himself on the tutorship. Master Blazius is the son's confessor, Master Bridaine the father's. I see them already, elbows on the table, cheeks in-flamed, eyes starting out of their heads, shaking their double chins in a paroxysm of hatred. They eye each other from head to foot; they begin the battle with petty skirmishes; soon war is declared; shots are exchanged; volleys of pedantry cross in midair; and, to cap all, between them frets Dame Pluche, repulsing them on either side with her sharp-pointed elbows... Now that dinner is over, the château gate is opened. The company are coming out; let us step aside out of the way. *(Exeunt.)*

(Enter the Baron and Dame Pluche.)

BARON. Venerable Pluche, I am pained.

PLUCHE. Is it possible, my lord?

BARON. Yes, Pluche, possible. I had calculated for a long time past—I had even set it down in black and white on my tablets that this day was to be the most enjoyable of my life. Yes, my good madame, the most enjoyable. You are not unaware that my plan was to marry my son to my niece. It was decided, arranged—I had mentioned it to Bridaine—and I see, I fancy I see, that these children speak to each other with coolness; they have not said a word to each other.

PLUCHE. There they come, my lord. Are they advised of your projects?

BARON. I dropped a few hints to each of them in private. I think it would be well, since they are thrown together now, that we should sit down under this propitious shade and leave them to themselves for a moment.

(He withdraws with Dame Pluche. Enter Camille and Perdican.)

11

PERDICAN. Do you know, Camille, it was not a bit nice of you to refuse me a kiss?

CAMILLE. I am always like that; it is my way.

PERDICAN. Will you take my arm for a stroll in the village?

CAMILLE. No, I am tired.

PERDICAN. Would it not please you to see the meadow again? Do you remember our boating excursions? Come, we will go down as far as the mill; I will take the oars, and you the tiller.

CAMILLE. I do not feel the least inclined for it.

PERDICAN. You cut me to the heart. What! not one remembrance, Camille? Not a heart-throb for our childhood, for all those kind, sweet past days, so full of delightful sillinesses? You will not come and see the path we used to go by to the farm?

CAMILLE. No, not this evening.

PERDICAN. Not this evening! But when? Our whole life lies there.

CAMILLE. I am not young enough to amuse myself with my dolls, nor old enough to love the past.

PERDICAN. What do you mean by that?

CAMILLE. I mean that recollections of childhood are not to my taste.

PERDICAN. They bore you?

CAMILLE. Yes, they bore me.

PERDICAN. Poor child; I am sincerely sorry for you.

(Exit in opposite directions.)

BARON *(entering with Dame Pluche).* You see and you hear, my excellent Pluche. I expected the softest harmony; and I feel as if I were attending a concert where the violin is playing "My heart it sighs," while the flute plays "Long live King Henry." Think of the frightful discord such a combination would produce! Yet that is what is going on in my heart.

PLUCHE. I must admit it is impossible for me to blame Camille, and to my mind nothing is in worse taste than boating excursions.

BARON. Are you serious?

PLUCHE. My lord, a young lady who respects herself does not risk herself on pieces of water.

BARON. But remark, pray Dame Pluche, that her cousin is to marry her, and that thenceforward—

PLUCHE. The proprieties forbid steering; and it is indelicate to leave *terra firma* alone with a young man.

BARON. But I repeat——I tell you

PLUCHE. That is my opinion—

BARON. Are you mad? Really you would make me say— There are certain expressions that I do not choose—that are repugnant to me. You make me want— Really, if I did not control myself— Pluche, you are a stupid person—— I do not know what to think of you. *(Exeunt.)*

SCENE IV

(A village green. The Chorus. Perdican.)

PERDICAN. Good day, friends; do you know me?

CHORUS. My lord, you are like a child we loved dearly.

PERDICAN. Was it not you who took me on your back to cross the streams of your meadows, who danced me on your knees, who took me up behind you on your sturdy horses, who crowded closer sometimes round your tables to make room for me at the farm supper?

CHORUS. We remember, my lord. You were certainly the naughtiest rogue and the finest boy on earth.

PERDICAN. Why do you not kiss me then, instead of saluting me like a stranger?

CHORUS. God bless you, child of our hearts. Each of us would like to take you in his arms; but we are old, my lord, and you are a man.

PERDICAN. Yes, it is ten years since I saw you; and in a single day all beneath the sun changes. I have grown some feet toward heaven; you have bowed some inches toward the grave. Your heads have whitened, your steps grown slower; you can no longer lift from the ground your child of long ago. So it is my turn now to be your father—father of you who were fathers to me.

CHORUS. Your return is a happier day than your birth. It is sweeter to recover what we love than to embrace a new-born babe.

PERDICAN. So this is my dear valley: my walnut-trees, my green paths, my little fountain. Here are my past days still full of life; here is the mysterious world of my childhood's dreams. Home, ah, home!—incomprehensible word. Can man be born just for a single corner of the earth, there to build his nest, and there to live his day?

CHORUS. We hear you are a learned man, my lord.

PERDICAN. Yes, I hear that too. Knowledge is a fine thing, lads. These trees and this meadow find a voice to teach the finest knowledge of all—how to forget what one knows.

CHORUS. There has been many a change during your absence. Girls are married, boys are gone to the army.

PERDICAN. You shall tell me all about it. I expect a deal of news; but to tell the truth, I do not care to hear it yet. How small this pool is; formerly it seemed immense. I had carried away an ocean and forests in my mind: I come back to find a drop of water and blades of grass. But who can that girl be, singing at her lattice behind those trees?

CHORUS. It is Rosette, your cousin Camille's foster-sister.

PERDICAN. *(stepping forward).* Come down quick, Rosette, and come here.

ROSETTE *(entering).* Yes, my lord.

PERDICAN. You saw me from your window, and you did not come, you wicked girl! Give me that hand of yours, quick now, and those cheeks to be kissed.

ROSETTE. Yes, my lord.

PERDICAN. Are you married, little one? They told me so.

ROSETTE. Oh, no!

PERDICAN. Why? There is not a prettier girl than you in the village. We'll find you a match, child.

CHORUS. My lord, she wants to die a maid.

PERDICAN. Is that true, Rosette?

ROSETTE. Oh, no!

PERDICAN. Your sister Camille is come! Have you seen her?

ROSETTE. She has not come this way yet.

PERDICAN. Be off quick, and put on your new dress, and come to supper at the château.

SCENE V

(A large room. Enter the Baron and Master Blazius.)

BLAZIUS. A word in your ear, my lord. The priest of your parish is a drunkard.

BARON. Shame! it is impossible.

BLAZIUS. I am certain of it. He drank three bottles of wine at dinner.

BARON. That is excessive.

BLAZIUS. And on leaving table he trampled on the flower-beds.

BARON. On the beds. You confound me. This is very strange. Drink three bottles of wine at dinner and trample on the flower-beds. Incomprehensible! And why did he not keep to the path?

BLAZIUS. Because he walked crooked.

BARON *(aside}*. I begin to think Bridaine was right. This fellow Blazius smells shockingly of wine.

BLAZIUS. Besides, he ate enormously; his utterance was thick.

BARON. Indeed I remarked that myself.

BLAZIUS. He delivered himself of a few Latin phrases; they were so many blunders. My lord, he is a depraved character.

BARON *(aside)*. Ugh! The odor of this fellow Blazius is past endurance. Understand, Mr. Tutor, that I am engaged with something very different from this, and that I do not concern myself with what is eaten or what is drunk here. I am not a major-domo.

BLAZIUS. Please God, I will never displease you, my lord. Your wine is good.

BARON. There is good wine in my cellars.

(Enter Master Bridaine.)

BRIDAINE. My lord, your son is out there on the green with all the ragamuffins of the village at his heels.

BARON. It is impossible.

BRIDAINE. I saw it with my own eyes. He was picking up pebbles to make ducks and drakes.

BARON. Ducks and drakes! My brain begins to reel. Here are all my ideas turning upside down. Bridaine, the report you bring me is absurd. It is unheard of that a Doctor of Laws should make ducks and drakes.

BRIDAINE. Go to the window, my lord; you will see with your own eyes.

BARON *(aside)*. Good heavens! Blazius was right. Bridaine walks crooked.

BRIDAINE. Look, my lord, there he is beside the pond. He has his arm round a peasant girl.

BARON. A peasant girl! Does my son come here to debauch my vassals? His arm round a peasant, and all the rowdies in the village round! I feel myself taking leave of my senses.

BRIDAINE. That calls for retribution.

BARON. All is lost irretrievably lost. I am lost. Bridaine staggers, Blazius reeks with wine, and my son seduces all the girls in the village while playing ducks and drakes. *(Exit.)*

ACT THE SECOND

SCENE I

(A garden. Enter Master Blazius and Perdican.)

BLAZIUS. My lord, your father is in despair.

PERDICAN. Why so?

BLAZIUS. You are aware that he had formed a plan of uniting you to your cousin Camille.

PERDICAN. Well, I ask no better!

BLAZIUS. Nevertheless, the Baron thinks he perceives an incompatibility in your characters.

PERDICAN. That is unlucky. I can not remodel mine.

BLAZIUS. Will you allow this to make the match impossible?

PERDICAN. I tell you once more I ask no better than to marry Camille. Go and find the Baron and tell him so.

BLAZIUS. My lord, I withdraw; here comes your cousin.

(Exit Blazius. Enter Camille.)

PERDICAN. Up already, cousin? I stick to what I said yesterday; you are ever so pretty!

CAMILLE. Let us be serious, Perdican. Your father wants to make a match between us. I do not know what you think of it, but I consider it right to forewarn you that I have made up my mind on the matter.

PERDICAN. The worse for me, if you dislike me.

CAMILLE. No more than any one else; I do not intend to marry. There is nothing in that to wound your pride!

PERDICAN. I do not deal in pride: I care for neither its joys nor its pains.

CAMILLE. I came here to enter on possession of my mother's property; to-morrow I go back to my convent.

PERDICAN. Well, you play fair. Shake hands and let us be good friends!

CAMILLE. I do not like demonstrations.

PERDICAN. *(taking her hand)*. Give me your hand, Camille, I beg of you. What do you fear of me? You do not choose that we should be married. Very well! let us not marry. Is that a reason for hating one another? Are we not brother and sister? When your mother enjoined this marriage in her will, she wished that our friendship should be unending, that is all she wished. Why marry? There is your hand, there is mine, and to keep them united thus to our last sigh, do you think we need a priest? We need none but God.

CAMILLE. I am very glad my refusal leaves you unconcerned.

PERDICAN. I am not unconcerned, Camille. Your love would have given me life, but your friendship shall console me for the lack of it. Do not leave the château to-morrow. Yesterday you refused to stroll round the garden with me, because you saw in me a husband you would not accept. Stay here a few days; let me hope that our past life is not dead for ever in your heart.

CAMILLE. I am bound to leave.

PERDICAN. Why?

CAMILLE. That is my secret.

PERDICAN. Do you love another?

CAMILLE. No; but I will go.

PERDICAN. Is it irrevocable?

CAMILLE. Yes, irrevocable.

PERDICAN. Well! adieu. I should have liked to sit with you under the chestnuts in the little wood, and chat like kind friends for an hour or two. But if you do not care for that, let us say no more. Good-by, my child.

(Exit Perdican. Enter Dame Pluche.)

CAMILLE. Is all ready, Dame Pluche? Shall we start to-morrow? Has my guardian finished his accounts?

PLUCHE. Yes, dear unspotted dove. The Baron called me a stupid person yesterday, and I am delighted to go.

CAMILLE. Stay; here is a line you will take to Lord Perdican, before dinner, from me.

PLUCHE. O, Lord of heaven! Is it possible? You writing a note to a man—

CAMILLE. Am I not to be his wife? Surely I may write to my fiancé.

PLUCHE. Lord Perdican has just left this spot. What can you have to write? Your fiancé; Heaven have pity on us! Can it be true that you are forgetting Jesus?

CAMILLE. Do what I tell you, and make all ready for my departure. *(Exeunt.)*

SCENE II

(The dining-room; servants setting the table. Enter Master Bridaine.)

BRIDAINE. Yes, it is a certainty, they will give him the place of honor again to-day. This chair on the Baron's right that I have filled so long will be the tutor's prize. Wretch that I am! A mechanical ass, a brazen drunkard gets me banished to the lower end of the table. The butler will pour for him the first glass of malaga, and when the dishes reach me they will be half cold; all the tit-bits will be eaten up; not a cabbage nor a carrot left round the partridges. Holy Catholic Church! To give him that place yesterday well that was intelligible. He had just arrived, and was sitting down to that table for the first time since many a long year. Heavens, how he drank! No, he will leave me nothing but bones and chicken's claws. I will not endure this affront. Farewell, venerable arm-chair in which many and many a time I have thrown my self back stuffed with juicy dishes! Farewell, sealed bottles; farewell matchless savor of venison done to a turn! Farewell, splendid board, noble dining-hall; I shall say grace here no longer. I return to my vicarage; they shall not see me confounded among the mob of guests; and, like Caesar, I will rather be first in the village than second in Rome.

SCENE III

(A field in front of a cottage. Enter Rosette and Perdican.)

PERDICAN. Since your mother is out, come for a little walk.

ROSETTE. Do you think all these kisses do me any good?

PERDICAN. What harm do you see in them? I would kiss you before your mother. Are you not Camille's sister? Am I not your brother just as I am hers?

ROSETTE. Words are words, and kisses are kisses. I am no better than a fool, and I find it out too, as soon as I have something to say. Fine ladies know what it means if you kiss their right hand, or if you kiss the left. Their fathers kiss them on the forehead; their mothers on the cheeks; and their lovers on the lips. Now everybody kisses me on both cheeks, and that vexes me.

PERDICAN. How pretty you are, child!

ROSETTE. All the same, you must not be angry with me for that. How sad you seem this morning! So your marriage is broken off?

PERDICAN. The peasants of your village remember they loved me; the dogs in the poultry yard and the trees in the wood remember it too; but Camille does not remember. And your marriage, Rosette—when is it to be?

ROSETTE. Do not let us talk of that, if you please? Talk of the weather, of the flowers here, of your horses, of my caps.

PERDICAN. Of whatever you please, of whatever can cross your lips without robbing them of that heavenly smile.

(He kisses her.)

ROSETTE. You respect my smile, but you do not spare my lips much, it seems to me. Why, do look; there is a drop of rain fallen on my hand, and yet the sky is clear.

PERDICAN. Forgive me.

ROSETTE. What have I done to make you weep? *(Exeunt.)*

SCENE IV

(The château. Enter Master Blazius and the Baron.)

BLAZIUS. My lord, I have a strange thing to tell you. A few minutes ago I chanced to be in the pantry—I mean in the gallery; what should I be doing in the pantry? Well, I was in the gallery. I had happened to find a decanter—I mean a jug of water. How was I to find a decanter in the gallery? Well, I was just drinking a drop of wine—I mean a glass of water—to pass the time, and I was looking out of the window between two flower vases that seemed to me to be in a modern style, though they are copied from the Etruscan.

BARON. What an intolerable manner of talking you have adopted, Blazius! Your speeches are inexplicable.

BLAZIUS. Listen to me, my lord; lend me a moment's attention. Well, I was looking out of the window. In Heaven's name, do not grow impatient. It concerns the honor of the family.

BARON. The family! This is incomprehensible. The honor of the family, Blazius? Do you know there are thirty-seven males of us, and nearly as many females, in Paris and in the country?

BLAZIUS. Allow me to continue. Whilst I was drinking a drop of wine—I mean a glass of water—to hasten tardy digestion, would you believe I saw Dame Pluche passing under the window out of breath?

BARON. Why out of breath, Blazius? That is unwonted.

BLAZIUS. And beside her, red with anger, your niece Camille.

BARON. Who red with anger—my niece or Dame Pluche?

BLAZIUS. Your niece, my lord.

BARON. My niece red with anger? It is unheard of! And how do you know it was with anger? She might have been red for a thousand reasons. No doubt she had been chasing butterflies in my flower-garden.

BLAZIUS. I can not be positive about that—that may be; but she was exclaiming with vigor, "Go! Find him. Do as you are bid! You are a fool! I will have it!" And she rapped with her fan the elbow of Dame Pluche, who gave a jump in the clover at each exclamation.

BARON. In the clover! And what did the governess reply to my niece's vagaries? for such conduct merits that description.

BLAZIUS. The governess replied: "I will not go! I did not find him. He is making love to the villagers, to silly girls. I am too old to begin to carry love-letters. Thank God, I have kept my hands clean up till now." And while she spoke she was crumpling up in her fingers a scrap of paper folded in four.

BARON. I do not understand at all; my ideas are becoming totally confused. What reason could Dame Pluche have for crumpling a paper folded in four, while she gave jumps in the clover? I can not lend credence to such enormities.

BLAZIUS. Do you not clearly understand, my lord, what that indicated?

BARON. No, upon my honor, my friend; no, I do not understand a word of it, good or bad. All this seems to be a piece of ill-regulated conduct, but equally devoid of motive and excuse.

BLAZIUS. It means that your niece has a clandestine correspondence.

BARON. What are you saying? Do you reflect of whom you are speaking? Weigh your words, Abbé!

BLAZIUS. I might weigh them in the heavenly scales that are to weigh my soul at the last judgment, without finding a single syllable of them that does not ring true. Your niece has a clandestine correspondence.

BARON. But reflect, my friend, that it is impossible.

BLAZIUS. Why should she have entrusted a letter to her governess? Why should she have exclaimed, "Find him!" while the other sulked and petted?

BARON. And to whom was this letter addressed?

BLAZIUS. That is exactly the question—the *hic jacet lepus*. To whom was this letter addressed? To a man who is making love to a silly girl. Now a man who publicly courts a silly girl may be evidently suspected of being himself born to herd geese. Nevertheless, it is impossible that your niece, with the education she has received, should be captivated by such a man. That is what I tell you, and that is why, saving your presence, I do not understand a word of it any more than you.

BARON. Good heavens! My niece declared to me this morning that she refused her cousin Perdican's hand. Can she be in love with a goose-herder? Step into my study. Since yesterday I have experienced such violent shocks that I can not collect my ideas. *(Exeunt.)*

SCENE V

(A fountain in a wood. Enter Perdican, reading a note.)

PERDICAN. "Be at the little fountain at noon." What does that mean? Such coldness; so positive and cruel a refusal; such unfeeling pride; and, to crown all, a rendezvous. If it is to talk business, why choose such a spot? Is it a piece of coquetry? This morning, as I walked with Rosette, I heard a stir in the brushwood. I thought it was a doe's tread. Is there some plot in this?

(Enter Camille.)

CAMILLE. Good day, cousin. I thought, rightly or wrongly, that you left me sadly this morning. You took my hand in spite of me. I come to ask you to give me yours. I refused you a kiss—here it is for you. *(Kissing him.)* Now then, you said you would like to have a friendly chat with me. Sit down then, and let us talk. *(She sits down.)*

PERDICAN. Was it a dream, or do I dream again now?

CAMILLE. You thought it odd to get a note from me, did you not? I am changeable; but you said one thing this morning that was very true: "Since we part, let us part good friends." You do not know the reason of my leaving, and I have come here to tell you. I am going to take the veil.

PERDICAN. Is it possible? Is it you, Camille, that I see reflected in this fountain, sitting on the daisies, as in the old days?

CAMILLE. Yes, Perdican, it is I. I have come to live over again one half-hour of the past life. I seemed to you rude and haughty. That is easily understood; I have renounced the world. Yet, before I leave it, I should like to hear your opinion. Do you think I am right to turn nun?

PERDICAN. Do not question me on the subject, for I shall never turn monk.

CAMILLE. In the ten years almost that we have lived separated from each other you have begun the experience of life. I know the man you are; and a heart and brain like yours must have learned much in a little while. Tell me, have you had mistresses?

PERDICAN. Why so?

CAMILLE. Answer me, I beg of you, without bashfulness and without affectation.

PERDICAN. I have had.

CAMILLE. Did you love them?

PERDICAN. With all my heart.

CAMILLE. Where are they now? Do you know?

PERDICAN. These are odd questions, upon my word. What would you have me say? I am neither their husband nor their brother. They went where it pleased them.

CAMILLE. There must needs have been one you preferred to all others. How long did you love the one you loved best?

PERDICAN. You are a queer girl. Do you want to turn father confessor?

CAMILLE. I ask of you as a favor to answer me sincerely. You are far from a libertine, and I believe that your heart is honest. You must have inspired love, for you are worth it; and you would not have abandoned yourself to a whim. Answer me, I beg.

PERDICAN. On my honor, I do not remember.

CAMILLE. Do you know a man who has loved only one woman?

PERDICAN. There are such, certainly.

CAMILLE. Is he one of your friends? Tell me his name.

PERDICAN. I have no name to tell you; but I believe there are men capable of loving once, and once only.

CAMILLE. How often can an honorable man love?

PERDICAN. Do you want to make me repeat a litany, or are you repeating a catechism yourself?

CAMILLE. I want to get information, and to learn whether I do right or wrong to take the veil. If I married you, would you not be bound to answer all my questions frankly, and lay your heart bare for me to see? I have a great regard for you, and I count you superior by nature and education to many other men. I am sorry you have forgotten the things I question you about. Perhaps if I knew you better I should grow bolder.

PERDICAN. What are you driving at? Go on. I will answer.

CAMILLE. Answer my first question then. Am I right to stay in the convent?

PERDICAN. No!

CAMILLE. Then I should do better to marry you?

PERDICAN. Yes.

CAMILLE. If the priest of your parish breathed on a glass of water, and told you it was a glass of wine, would you drink it as such?

PERDICAN. No!

CAMILLE. If the priest of your parish breathed on you, and told me that you would love all your life, should I do right to believe him?

PERDICAN. Yes, and no.

CAMILLE. What would you advise me to do the day I saw you loved me no longer?

PERDICAN. To take a lover.

CAMILLE. What shall I do next the day my lover loves me no longer?

PERDICAN. Take another.

CAMILLE. How long will that go on?

PERDICAN. Till your hairs are gray, and then mine will be white.

CAMILLE. Do you know what the cloisters are, Perdican? Did you ever sit a whole day long on the bench of a nunnery?

PERDICAN. Yes, I have.

CAMILLE. I have a friend, a sister, thirty years old, who at fifteen had an income of five hundred thousand crowns. She is the most beautiful and noble creature that ever walked on earth. She was a peeress of the parliament, and had for a husband one of the most distinguished men in France. Not one of the faculties that ennoble humanity had been left uncultivated in her, and like a sapling of some choice stock all her buds had branched. Love and happiness will never set their crown of flowers on a fairer forehead. Her husband deceived her; she loved another man, and she is dying of despair.

PERDICAN. That is possible.

CAMILLE. We share the same cell, and I have passed whole nights in talking of her sorrows. They have almost become mine: that is strange, is it not? I do not quite know how it comes to pass. When she spoke to me of her marriage, when she painted the intoxication of the first days, and then the tranquility of the rest, and how at last the whole had taken wings and flown; how in the evening she sat down at the chimney-corner, and he by the window, without a word said between them; how their love had languished, and how every effort to draw close again only ended in quarrels; how little by little a strange figure came and placed itself between them, and glided in amid their sufferings; it was still myself that I saw acting while she spoke. When she said, "There I was happy," my heart leaped; when she added, "There I wept," my tears flowed. But fancy a thing stranger still. I ended by creating an imaginary life for myself. It lasted four years. It is needless to tell by how many reflected lights, how many doublings on myself all this came about. What I wanted to tell you as a curiosity is that all Louise's tales, all the phantoms of my dreams, bore your likeness.

PERDICAN. My likeness—mine?

CAMILLE. Yes—and that is natural; you were the only man I had known. In all truth I loved you, Perdican.

PERDICAN. How old are you, Camille?

CAMILLE. Eighteen.

PERDICAN. Go on, go on; I am listening.

CAMILLE. There are two hundred women in our convent. A small number of these women will never know life; all the rest are waiting for death. More than one of them left the convent as I leave it to-day, virgin and full of hopes. They returned after a little while old and blasted. Every day some of them die in our dormitories, and every day fresh ones come to take the place of the dead on the hair mattresses. Strangers who visit us admire the calm and order of the house; they look attentively at the whiteness of our veils; but they ask themselves why we lower them over our eyes. What do you think of these women, Perdican? Are they wrong or are they right?

PERDICAN. I can not tell.

CAMILLE. There were some of them who counseled me to remain unmarried. I am glad to be able to consult you. Do you believe these women would have done better to take a lover, and counsel me to do the same?

PERDICAN. I can not tell.

CAMILLE. You promised to answer me.

PERDICAN. I am absolved, as a matter of course, from the promise. I do not believe it is you who are speaking.

CAMILLE. That may be; there must be great absurdities in all my ideas. It may well be that I have learned by rote, that I am only an ill-taught parrot. In the gallery there is a little picture that represents a monk bending over a missal; through the gloomy bars of his cell slides a feeble ray of sunlight, and you catch sight of an Italian inn, in front of which dances a goatherd. Which of these two men has more of your esteem?

PERDICAN. Neither one nor the other, and both. They are two men of flesh and blood; there is one that reads and one that dances; I see nothing else in it. You are right to turn nun.

CAMILLE. A minute ago you told me no.

PERDICAN. Did I say no? That is possible.

CAMILLE. So you advise me to do it?

PERDICAN. So you believe in nothing?

CAMILLE. Lift your head, Perdican. Who is the man that believes in nothing?

PERDICAN. *(rising).* Here is one: I do not believe in immortal life. My darling sister, the nuns have given you their experience, but believe me it is not yours; you will not die without loving.

CAMILLE. I want to love, but I do not want to suffer. I want to love with an undying love, and to swear vows that are not broken. Here is my lover. *(Showing her crucifix.)*

PERDICAN. That lover does not exclude others.

CAMILLE. For me, at least, he shall exclude them. Do not smile, Perdican. It is ten years since I saw you, and I go to-morrow. In ten years more, if we meet again, we will again speak of this. I did not wish your memory to picture me as a cold statue; for lack of feeling leads to the point I have reached. Listen to me. Return to life; and so long as you are happy, so long as you love as men can love on earth, forget your sister Camille; but if ever it chances to you to be forgotten, or yourself to forget; if the angel of hope abandons you when you are alone, with emptiness in your heart, think of me, who shall be praying for you.

PERDICAN. You are a proud creature; take care of yourself.

CAMILLE. Why?

PERDICAN. You are eighteen, and you do not believe in love.

CAMILLE. Do you believe in it, you who speak to me? There you are, bending beside me knees that have worn themselves on the carpets of your mistresses, whose very names you forget. You have wept tears of joy and tears of despair; but you knew that the spring water was more constant than your tears, and would be always there to wash your swollen eyelids. You follow your vocation of young man, and you smile when one speaks to you of women's lives blasted; you do not believe that love can kill, since you have loved and live. What is the world then? It seems to me that you must cordially despise the women who take you as you are, and who dismiss their last lover to draw you to their arms with another's kisses on their lips. A moment ago I was asking you if you had loved. You answered me like a traveler whom one might ask had he been in Italy or in Germany, and who should say, "Yes, I have been there;" then should think of going to Switzerland or the first country you may name. Is your love a coinage then, that it can pass like this from hand to hand till the day of death? No, not even a coin; for the tiniest gold piece is better than you, and whatever hand it may pass to, still keeps its stamp.

PERDICAN. How beautiful you are, Camille, when your eyes grow bright!

CAMILLE. Yes, I am beautiful; I know it. Compliment-mongers will teach me nothing new. The cold nun who cuts my hair off will perhaps turn pale at her work of mutilation; but it shall not change into rings and chains to go the round of the boudoirs. Not a strand of it shall be missing from my head when the steel passes there. I ask only one snap of the scissors, and when the conescrating priest draws on my finger the gold ring of my heavenly spouse, the tress of hair I give him may serve him for a cloak.

PERDICAN. Upon my word, you are angry.

CAMILLE. I did wrong to speak; my whole life is on my lips. Oh, Perdican, do not scoff; it is all deathly sad.

PERDICAN. Poor child, I let you speak, and I have a good mind to answer you one word. You speak to me of a nun who appears to me to have a disastrous influence upon you. You say that she has been deceived, that she herself has been false, and that she is in despair. Are you sure that if her husband or her lover came back, and stretched his hand to her through the grating of the convent parlor, she would not give him hers?

CAMILLE. What do you say? I did not understand.

PERDICAN. Are you sure that if her husband or her lover came, and bade her suffer again, she would answer, no?

CAMILLE. I believe it.

PERDICAN. There are two hundred women in your convent, and most of them have in the recesses of their hearts deep wounds. They have made you touch them, and they have dyed your maiden thoughts with drops of their blood. They have lived, have they not? And they have shown you shudderingly their life's road. You have crossed yourself before their scars as you would before the wounds of Jesus. They have made a place for you in their doleful processions, and you press closer to these fleshless bodies with a religious dread when you see a man pass. Are you sure that if the man passing were he who deceived them, he for whom they weep and suffer, he whom they curse as they pray to God—are you sure that at sight of him they would not burst their fetters to fly to their past misfortunes, and to press their bleeding breasts against the poniard that scarred them? Oh, child! do you know the dreams of these women who tell you not to dream? Do you know what name they murmur when the sighs issuing from their lips shake the sacramental host as it is offered to them? These women who sit down by you with swaying heads to pour into your ear the poison of their tarnished age, who clang among the ruins of your youth the tocsin of their despair, and strike into your crimson blood the chill of their tombs, do you know who they are?

CAMILLE. You frighten me. Anger is gaining upon you too.

PERDICAN. Do you know what nuns are, unhappy girl? Do they who represent to you men's love as a lie, know that there is a worse thing still the lie of a divine love? Do they know that they commit a crime when they come whispering to a maiden, woman's talk? Ah! how they have schooled you! How clearly I divined all this when you stopped before the portrait of our old aunt! You wanted to go without pressing my hand; you would not revisit this wood, nor this poor little fountain that looks at us bathed in tears; you were a renegade to the days of your childhood, and the mask of plaster the nuns have placed on your cheeks refused me a brother's kiss. But your heart beat; it forgot its lesson, for it has not learned to read, and you returned to sit on this turf where now we are. Well, Camille, these women said well. They put you in the right path. It may cost me my life's happiness, but tell them from me—heaven is not for them.

CAMILLE. Nor for me, is it?

PERDICAN. Farewell, Camille. Return to your convent; and when they tell you one of their hideous stories that have poisoned your nature, give them the answer: "All men are liars, fickle, chatterers, hypocrites, proud or cowardly, despicable, sensual; all women faithless, tricky, vain, inquisitive, and depraved." The world is only a bottomless cesspool, where the most shapeless sea-beasts climb and writhe on mountains of slime. But there is in the world a thing holy and sublime the union of two of these beings, imperfect and frightful as they are. One is often deceived in love, often wounded, often unhappy; but one loves, and on the brink of the grave one turns to look back and says: I have suffered often, sometimes I have been mistaken, but I have loved. It is I who have lived, and not a spurious being bred of my pride and my sorrow. *(Exit.)*

ACT THE THIRD

SCENE I

(The front of the château. Enter the Baron and Master Blazius.)

BARON. Independently of your drunkenness, you are a worthless fellow, Master Blazius. My servants see you enter the pantry furtively; and when you are accused of having stolen my wine, in the most pitiable manner you think to justify yourself by accusing my niece of a clandestine correspondence.

BLAZIUS. But, my lord, pray remember

BARON. Leave the house, Abbe, and never appear before me again. It is unreasonable to act as you do, and my self-respect constrains me never to pardon you as long as I live.

(Exit Baron. Master Blazius follows. Enter Perdican.)

PERDICAN. I should like to know if I am in love. On the one hand, there is that fashion of questioning me, a trifle bold for a girl of eighteen. On the other, the ideas that these nuns have stuffed into her head will not be set right without trouble. Besides, she is to go to-day. Confound it! I love her; there is not a doubt of it. After all, who knows? Perhaps she was repeating a lesson; and besides, it is clear she does not trouble her head about me. On the other hand again, her prettiness is all very well; but that does not alter the fact that she has much too decided a manner and too curt a tone. My only plan is to think no more of it. It is plain I do not love her. There is no doubt she is pretty; but why can I not put yesterday's talk out of my head? Upon my word, my wits were wandering all last night. Now where am I going? Ah, I am going to the village. *(Exit.)*

SCENE II

(A road. Enter Master Bridaine.)

BRIDAINE. What are they doing now? Alas! there is twelve o'clock. They are at table. What are they eating? What are they not eating?

I saw the cook cross the village with a huge turkey. The scullion carried the truffles, with a basket of grapes.

(Enter Master Blazius.)

BLAZIUS. Oh, unforeseen disgrace! here I am turned out of the château, and, in consequence, from the dinner-table. I shall never drink the wine in the pantry again.

BRIDAINE. I shall never see the dishes smoke again. Never again before the blaze of that noble hearth shall I warm my capacious belly.

BLAZIUS. Why did a fatal curiosity prompt me to listen to the conversation between Dame Pluche and the niece? Why did I report all I saw to the Baron?

BRIDAINE. Why did an idle pride remove me from that honorable dinner when I was so kindly welcomed? What mattered to me the seat on the right or seat on the left?

BLAZIUS. Alas! I was tipsy, it must be admitted, when I committed this folly.

BRIDAINE. Alas! the wine had mounted to my head when I was guilty of this rashness.

BLAZIUS. Yonder is the Vicar, I think.

BRIDAINE. It is the tutor in person.

BLAZIUS. Oh! oh! Vicar, what are you doing here?

BRIDAINE. I? I am going to dinner. Are you not coming?

BLAZIUS. Alas, Master Bridaine, intercede for me; the Baron has dismissed me. I falsely accused Mademoiselle Camille of having a clandestine correspondence; and yet, God is my witness that I saw, or thought I saw, Dame Pluche in the clover. I am ruined, Vicar.

BRIDAINE. What do you tell me?

BLAZIUS. Alas! alas! the truth. I am in utter disgrace for stealing a bottle.

BRIDAINE. What has this talk of stolen bottles to do, sir, with a clover patch and correspondence?

BLAZIUS. I entreat you to plead my cause. I am honorable, my Lord Bridaine. O, worshipful Lord Bridaine, I am yours to command.

BRIDAINE. O, fortune! is it a dream? Shall I then be seated on yon blessed chair?

BLAZIUS. I shall be grateful to you would you hear my story and kindly excuse me, your worship, my dear Vicar.

BRIDAINE. That is impossible, sir; it has struck twelve, and I am off to dinner. If the Baron complains of you, that is your business.

I do not intercede for a sot. *(Aside.)* Quick, fly to the gate: swell, my stomach. *(Exit running.)*

BLAZIUS. *(alone).* Wretched Pluche! it is you shall pay for them all; yes, it is you are the cause of my ruin, shameless woman, vile go-between, it is to you I owe my disgrace. Holy University of Paris! I am called sot! I am undone if I do not get hold of a letter, and if I do not prove to the Baron that his niece has a correspondence. I saw her writing at her desk this morning. Patience! here comes news!

(Dame Pluche passes carrying a letter.)

BLAZIUS. Pluche, give me that letter.

PLUCHE. What is the meaning of this? It is a letter of my mistress's that I am going to post in the village.

BLAZIUS. Give it to me, or you are a dead woman.

PLUCHE. I dead! Dead?

BLAZIUS. Yes, dead, Pluche; give me that paper.

(They fight. Enter Perdican.)

PERDICAN. What is this? What are you about, Blazius? Why are you molesting this woman?

PLUCHE. Give me back the letter. He took it from me, my lord. Justice!

BLAZIUS. She is a go-between, my lord. That letter is a billet-doux.

PLUCHE. It is a letter of Camille's, my lord—your fiancée's.

BLAZIUS. It is a billet-doux to a gooseherder.

PLUCHE. You lie, Abbé. Let me tell you that.

PERDICAN. Give me that letter. I understand nothing about your quarrel; but as Camille's fiancé, I claim the right to read it. *(Reads.)* "To Sister Louise, at the Convent of—." Leave me, Dame Pluche; you are a worthy woman, and Master Blazius is a fool. Go to dinner; I undertake to put this letter in the post.

(Exeunt Master Blazius and Dame Pluche.)

PERDICAN. *(alone).* That it is a crime to open a letter I know too well to be guilty of it. What can Camille be saying to this sister? Am I in love after all? What empire has this strange girl gained over me that the line of writing on this address should make my

33

hand shake? That's odd; Blazius in his struggle with Dame Pluche has burst the seal. Is it a crime to unfold it? No matter, I will put everything just as it was. *(Opens the letter and reads.)* "I am leaving today, my dear, and all has happened as I had foreseen. It is a terrible thing; but that poor young man has a dagger in his heart; he will never be consoled for having lost me. Yet I have done everything in the world to disgust him with me. God will pardon me for having reduced him to despair by my refusal. Alas! my dear, what could I do? Pray for me; we shall meet again to-morrow, and forever. Yours with my whole soul. Camille." Is it possible? That is how Camille writes! That is how she speaks of me! I in despair at her refusal! Oh! Good heavens, if that were true it would be easily seen; what shame could there be in loving? She does everything in the world, she says, to disgust me, and I have a dagger in my heart. What reason can she have to invent such a romance? Is it then true the thought that I had to-night? Oh, women! This poor Camille has great piety perhaps. With a willing heart she gives herself to God, but she has resolved and decreed that she would leave me in despair. That was settled between the two friends before she left the convent. It was decided that Camille was going to see her cousin again, that they would wish her to marry him, that she would refuse, and that the cousin would be in despair. It is so interesting for a young girl to sacrifice to God the happiness of a cousin! No, no, Camille, I do not love you, I am not in despair, I have not a dagger in my heart, and I will prove it to you. Yes, before you leave this you shall know that I love another. Here, my good man!

(Enter a peasant.)

PERDICAN. Go to the château; tell them in the kitchen to send a servant to take this note to Mademoiselle Camille. *(He writes.)*

PEASANT. Yes, my lord. *(He goes out.)*

PERDICAN. Now for the other. Ah! I am in despair. Here! Rosette, Rosette!

(He knocks at a door.)

ROSETTE. *(opening it).* Is it you, my lord? Come in, my mother is here.

PERDICAN. Put on your prettiest cap, Rosette, and come with me.

ROSETTE. Where?

PERDICAN. I will tell you. Ask leave of your mother, but make haste.
ROSETTE. Yes, my lord.

(She goes into the house.)

PERDICAN. I have asked Camille for another rendezvous, and I am sure she will come; but, by Heaven, she will not find what she expects there. I mean to make love to Rosette before Camille herself.

SCENE III

(The little wood. Enter Camille and the peasant.)

PEASANT. I am going to the château with a letter for you, mademoiselle. Must I give it to you, or must I leave it in the kitchen, as Lord Perdican told me?
CAMILLE. Give it me.
PEASANT. If you would rather I took it to the château, it is not worth while waiting here.
CAMILLE. Give it me, I tell you.
PEASANT. As you please. *(Gives the letter.)*
CAMILLE. Stop. There is for your trouble.
PEASANT. Much obliged. I may go, may I not?
CAMILLE. If you like.
PEASANT. I am going, I am going. *(Exit.)*
CAMILLE. *(reading).* Perdican asks me to say good-by to him before leaving, near the little fountain where I brought him yesterday. What can he have to say to me? Why, here is the fountain, and I am on the spot. Ought I to grant this second rendezvous? Ah! *(Hides behind a tree.)* There is Perdican coming this way with my foster-sister. I suppose he will leave her. I am glad that I shall not seem to be the first to arrive.

(Enter Perdican and Rosette and sit down.)

CAMILLE. *(hidden, aside).* What is the meaning of this? He is making her sit down beside him. Does he ask me for a rendezvous to come there and talk with another girl? I am curious to know what he says to her.

PERDICAN. *(aloud, so that Camille hears).* I love you, Rosette. You alone, out of all the world, have forgotten nothing of our good days that are past. You are the only one who remembers the life that is no more. Share my new life. Give me your heart, sweet child. There is the pledge of our love. *(Putting his chain on her neck.)*

ROSETTE. Are you giving me your gold chain?

PERDICAN. Now look at this ring. Stand up and let us come near the fountain. Do you see us both in the spring leaning on each other? Do you see your lovely eyes near mine, your hand in mine? Watch how all that is blotted out. *(Throwing his ring into the water.)* Look how our image has disappeared. There it is coming back little by little. The troubled water regains its tranquility. It trembles still. Great black rings float over its surface. Patience. We are reappearing. Already I can make out again your arms entwined in mine. One minute more and there will not be a wrinkle left in your pretty face. Look! It was a ring that Camille gave me.

CAMILLE. *(aside).* He has thrown my ring into the water.

PERDICAN. Do you know what love is, Rosette? Listen! the wind is hushed; the morning rain runs pearling over the parched leaves that the sun revives. By the light of heaven, by this sun we see, I love you! You will have me, will you not? No one has tarnished your youth! No one has distilled into your crimson blood the dregs of jaded veins! You do not want to turn nun? There you stand, young and fair, in a young man's arms. O, Rosette, Rosette, do you know what love is?

ROSETTE. Alas, Doctor, I will love you as best I can.

PERDICAN. Yes, as best you can; and that will be better, doctor though I am, and peasant though you are, than these pale statues can love, fashioned by nuns, their heads where their hearts should be, who leave the cloisters to come and spread through life the damp atmosphere of their cells. You know nothing; you could not read in a book the prayer that your mother taught you as she learned it from her mother. You do not even understand the sense of the words you repeat when you kneel at your bedside; but you understand that you are praying, and that is all God wants.

ROSETTE. How speak you, my lord!

PERDICAN. You can not read; but you can tell what these woods and meadows say, their warm rivers and fair harvest-covered fields, and all this nature radiant with youth. You recognize all these thousands of brothers and me as one of them. Rise up; you shall be my wife, and together we shall strike root into the vital currents of the almighty world.

SCENE IV

(Enter the Chorus.)

CHORUS. Certainly there is something strange going on at the château. Camille has refused to marry Perdican. She is to return to the convent from which she came. But I think his lordship, her cousin, has consoled himself with Rosette. Alas! the poor girl does not know the risk she runs in listening to the speeches of a gallant young nobleman.

(Enter Dame Pluche.)

PLUCHE. Quick! quick! saddle my ass.

CHORUS. Will you pass away like a beautiful dream, venerable lady? Are you going to bestride anew so soon that poor beast who is so sad to bear your weight?

PLUCHE. Thank God, my sweet rabble, I shall not die here!

CHORUS. Die far from here, Pluche, my darling; die unknown in some unwholesome cavern. We will pray for your worshipful resurrection.

PLUCHE. Here comes my mistress. *(To Camille, who enters.)* Dear Camille, all is ready for our start; the Baron has rendered his account, and they have pack-saddled my ass.

CAMILLE. Go to the devil, you and your ass too! I shall not start to-day. *(Exit.)*

CHORUS. What can this mean? Dame Pluche is pale with anger; her false hair tries to stand on end, her chest whistles, and her fingers stretch out convulsively.

PLUCHE. Lord, God of heaven! Camille swore!

(Exit Pluche.)

SCENE V

(Enter the Baron and Master Bridaine.)

BRIDAINE. My lord, I must speak to you in private. Your son is making love to a village girl.

BARON. It is absurd, my friend.

BRIDAINE. I distinctly saw him passing in the heather with her on his arm. He was bending his head to her ear and promising to marry her.

BARON. This is monstrous.

BRIDAINE. You may be convinced of it. He made her a considerable present that the girl showed her mother.

BARON. Heavens, Bridaine, considerable? In what way considerable?

BRIDAINE. In weight and importance. It was the gold chain he used to wear in his cap.

BARON. Let us step into my study. I do not know what to think of it. *(Exeunt.)*

SCENE VI

(Camille's room. Enter Camille and Dame Pluche.)

CAMILLE. He took my letter, you say?

PLUCHE. Yes, my child; he undertook to put it in the post.

CAMILLE. Go to the drawing-room, Dame Pluche, and do me the kindness to tell Perdican that I expect him here.

(Exit Dame Pluche.)

CAMILLE. He read my letter, that is a certainty. His scene in the wood was a retaliation, like his love for Rosette. He wished to prove to me that he loved another girl, and to play at unconcern in spite of his vexation. Could he be in love with me by any chance? *(She lifts the tapestry.)* Are you there, Rosette?

ROSETTE. *(entering).* Yes; may I come in?

CAMILLE. Listen to me, my child. Is not Lord Perdican making love to you?

ROSETTE. Alas! yes.

CAMILLE. What do you think of what he said to you this morning?

ROSETTE. This morning? Where?

CAMILLE. Do not play the hypocrite. This morning at the fountain in the little wood.

ROSETTE. You saw me there?

CAMILLE. Poor innocent! No, I did not see you. He made you fine speeches, did he not? I would wager he promised to marry you.

ROSETTE. How do you know that?

CAMILLE. What matter how? I know it. Do you believe in his promises, Rosette?

ROSETTE. Why, how could I help it? He deceive me? Why should he?

CAMILLE. Perdican will not marry you, my child.

ROSETTE. Alas! I can not tell.

CAMILLE. You are in love with him, poor girl. He will not marry you; and for proof, you shall have it. Go behind this curtain. You need only keep your ears open, and come when I call you.

(Exit Rosette.)

CAMILLE. *(alone).* Can it be that I, who thought I was doing an act of vengeance, am doing an act of humanity? The poor girl's heart is caught.

(Enter Perdican.)

CAMILLE. Good morning, cousin. Please sit down.

PERDICAN. What a toilette, Camille? Whose scalp are you after?

CAMILLE. Yours perhaps. I am sorry I could not come to the rendezvous you asked for; had you anything to say to me?

PERDICAN. *(aside).* A good-sized fib that, on my life, for a spotless lamb. I saw her listening to the conversation behind a tree. *(Aloud.)* I have nothing to say to you but a farewell, Camille. I thought you were starting; yet your horse is in the stable, and you do not look as if you were dressed for traveling.

CAMILLE. I like discussion. I am not very sure that I did not want to quarrel with you again.

PERDICAN. What is the use in quarreling when it is impossible to make friends again? The pleasure of disputes is in making peace.

CAMILLE. Are you convinced that I do not wish to make it?

PERDICAN. Do not laugh at me; I am no match for you there.

CAMILLE. I should like a flirtation. I do not know whether it is that I have a new dress on, but I want to amuse myself. You proposed going to the village; let us go. I am ready; let us take the boat. I want to picnic on the grass, or to take a stroll in the forest. Will it be moonlight this evening? That is odd; you have not the ring I gave you on your finger.

PERDICAN. I have lost it.

CAMILLE. Then that is why I found it. There, Perdican; here it is for you.

PERDICAN. Is it possible? Where did you find it?

CAMILLE. You are looking to see if my hands are wet, are you not? Indeed, I spoiled my convent dress to get this little child's plaything out of the fountain. That is why I have put on another, and I tell you it has changed me. Come, put that on your finger.

PERDICAN. You got this ring out of the water, Camille, at the risk of falling in yourself. Is this a dream? There it is. It is you who are putting it on my finger. Ah, Camille, why do you give it me back, this sad pledge of a happiness that exists no longer? Speak, coquette; speak, rash girl. Why do you go? Why do you stay? Why do you change aspect and color from hour to hour, like the stone of this ring at every ray of the sun?

CAMILLE. Do you know the heart of women, Perdican? Are you sure of their inconstancy, and do you know whether they really change in thought when they change in words sometimes? Some say no. Undoubtedly we often have to play a part, often lie. You see I am frank. But are you sure that the whole woman lies when her tongue lies? Have you reflected well on the nature of this weak and passionate being, on the sternness with which she is judged, and on the rules that are imposed on her? And who knows whether, forced by the world into deceit, this little brainless being's head may not take a pleasure in it, and lie sometimes for pastime or for folly, as she does for necessity?

PERDICAN. I understand nothing of all this, and I never lie. I love you, Camille. That is all I know.

CAMILLE. You say that you love me, and that you never lie—

PERDICAN. Never.

CAMILLE. Yet here is one who says that that sometimes happens to you.

(She raises the tapestry. Rosette is seen in the distance fainting on a chair.)

CAMILLE. What answer will you make to this child, Perdican, when she demands an account of your words? If you never lie, how comes it then that she fainted on hearing you tell me that you love me? I leave you with her. Try to restore her.

(She attempts to leave.)

PERDICAN. One moment, Camille. Listen to me.

CAMILLE. What would you tell me? It is to Rosette you should speak. I do not love you. I did not go out of spite and fetch this unhappy child from the shelter of her cottage, to make a bait and a plaything of her. I did not rashly repeat before her burning words addressed to another woman. I did not feign to hurl to the winds for her sake the remembrance of a cherished friendship. I did not put my chain on her neck. I did not tell her I would marry her.

PERDICAN. Listen to me, listen to me.

CAMILLE. Did you not smile a moment ago when I told you I had not been able to go to the fountain? Well. Yes, I was there, and I heard all. But God is my witness, I would not care to have spoken as you spoke there. What will you do with that girl yonder, now when she comes with your passionate kisses on her lips and shows you, weeping, the wound you have dealt her? You wished to be revenged on me did you not? and to punish me for a letter written to my convent. You wished to loosen, at whatever cost, any shaft that could reach me, and you counted it as nothing to pierce this child with your poisoned arrow, provided it struck me behind her. I had boasted of having inspired some love in you, of leaving you some regret for me. So that wounded you in your noble pride! Well, learn it from my lips. You love me do you hear? but you will marry that girl, or you are a coward.

PERDICAN. Yes, I will marry her.

CAMILLE. And you will do well.

PERDICAN. Right well and far better than if I married you yourself. Why so hot, Camille? This child has fainted. We shall easily restore her. A flask of vinegar is all that is needed. You wished to prove to me that I had lied once in my life. That is possible, but I think you are bold to determine at what moment. Come, help me to aid Rosette.

(Exeunt.)

SCENE VII

(The Baron and Camille.)

BARON. If that takes place, I shall run mad.

CAMILLE. Use your authority.

BARON. I shall run mad, and I shall refuse my consent, that's certain.

CAMILLE. You ought to speak to him, and make him listen to reason.

BARON. This will throw me into despair for the whole carnival, and I shall not appear once at court. It is a disproportioned marriage. Nobody ever heard of marrying one's cousin's foster-sister; that passes all kinds of bounds.

CAMILLE. Send for him, and tell him flatly that you do not like the marriage. Believe me, it is a piece of madness, and he will not resist.

BARON. I shall be in black this winter, be assured of that.

CAMILLE. But speak to him, in Heaven's name. This is a freak of his; perhaps it is too late already; if he has spoken of it, he will carry it out.

BARON. I am going to shut myself up, that I may abandon myself to my sorrow. Tell him, if he asks for me, that I have shut myself up, and that I am abandoning myself to my sorrow at seeing him wed a nameless girl. *(Exit.)*

CAMILLE. Shall I not find a man of sense here? Upon my word, when you look for one, the solitude becomes appalling.

(Enter Perdican.)

CAMILLE. Well, cousin, and when is the wedding to be?

PERDICAN. As soon as possible; I have mentioned it already to the notary, the priest, and all the peasants.

CAMILLE. You really think, then, that you will marry Rosette?

PERDICAN. Assuredly.

CAMILLE. What will your father say?

PERDICAN. Whatever he pleases; I choose to marry this girl; it is an idea for which I am indebted to you, and I stand to it. Need I repeat to you the hackneyed commonplaces about my birth and hers? She is young and pretty, and she loves me; it is more than one needs to be trebly happy. Whether she has brains or not, I might have found worse. People will raise an outcry, and a laugh; I wash my hands of them.

CAMILLE. There is nothing laughable in it; you do very well to marry her. But I am sorry for you on one account: people will say you married her out of spite.

PERDICAN. You sorry for that? Oh, no!

CAMILLE. Yes, I am really sorry for it. It injures a young man to be unable to resist a moment's annoyance.

PERDICAN. Be sorry then; for my part, it is all one to me.

CAMILLE. But you do not mean it; she is nobody.

PERDICAN. She will be somebody then, when she is my wife.

CAMILLE. You will tire of her before the notary has put on his best coat and his shoes, to come here; your gorge will rise at the wedding breakfast, and the evening of the ceremony you will have her hands and feet cut off, as they do in the "Arabian Nights," because she smells of *ragout*.

PERDICAN. No such thing, you will see. You do not know me. When a woman is gentle and affectionate, fresh, kind, and beautyful, I am capable of contenting myself with that; yes, upon my word, even to the length of not caring to know if she speaks Latin.

CAMILLE. It is a pity there was so much money spent on teaching it to you: it is three thousand crowns lost.

PERDICAN. Yes; they would have done better to give it to the poor.

CAMILLE. You will take charge of it, for the poor in spirit, at least.

PERDICAN. And they will give me in exchange the kingdom of heaven, for it is theirs.

CAMILLE. How long will this sport last?

PERDICAN. What sport?

CAMILLE. Your marriage with Rosette.

PERDICAN. A very little while: God has not made man a lasting piece of work: thirty or forty years at the most.

CAMILLE. I look forward to dancing at your wedding.

PERDICAN. Listen to me, Camille, this tone of raillery is out of place.

CAMILLE. I like it too well to leave it.

PERDICAN. Then I leave you, for I have enough of you for the moment.

CAMILLE. Are you going to your bride's home?

PERDICAN. Yes, this instant.

CAMILLE. Give me your arm; I am going there too.

(Enter Rosette.)

PERDICAN. Here you are, my child. Come, I want to present you to my father.

ROSETTE. *(kneeling down)*. My lord, I am come to ask a favor of you. All the village people I spoke to this morning told me that you loved your cousin, and that you only made love to me to amuse both of you; I am laughed at as I pass, and I shall not be able to find a husband in the country, now that I have been the laughing-stock of the neighborhood. Allow me to give you the necklace you gave me, and to live in peace with my mother.

CAMILLE. You are a good girl, Rosette; keep the necklace. It is I who give it you, and my cousin will take mine in its place. As for a husband, do not trouble your head for that; I undertake to find one for you.

PERDICAN. Certainly there is no difficulty about that. Come, Rosette, come and let me take you to my father.

CAMILLE. Why? It is useless.

PERDICAN. Yes, you are right; my father would receive us ill; we must let the first moment of his surprise pass by. Come with me; we will go back to the green. A good joke indeed that it should be said I do not love you, when I am marrying you. By Jove, we will silence them.

(Exit with Rosette.)

CAMILLE. What can be happening in me? He takes her away with a very tranquil air. That is odd; my head seems to be swimming. Could he marry her in good earnest? Ho! Dame Pluche, Dame Pluche! Is no one here?

(Enter a footman.)

CAMILLE. Run after Lord Perdican; make haste, and tell him to come here again, I want to speak to him.

(Exit footman.)

CAMILLE. What in the world is all this? I can bear no more; my feet refuse to support me.

(Re-enter Perdican.)

PERDICAN. You asked for me, Camille?
CAMILLE. No—no—
PERDICAN. Truly you are pale; what have you to say to me? You recalled me to speak to me.
CAMILLE. No—no— O, Lord God! *(Exit.)*

LAST SCENE

(An oratory. Enter Camille. She throws herself at the foot of the altar.)

CAMILLE. Have you abandoned me, O, my God? You know when I came here I had promised to be faithful to you. When I refused to become the bride of another than you, I thought I spoke in singleness of heart, before you and before my conscience. You know it, O, my Father! Do not reject me now. Ah, why do you make truth itself a liar? Why am I so weak? Ah, unhappy girl that I am; I can pray no more!

(Enter Perdican.)

PERDICAN. Pride, most fatal of men's counselors, why didst thou come between this girl and me? Yonder is she, pale and affrighted, pressing on the unfeeling stone her heart and her face. She might have loved me. We were born for one another. Wherefore earnest thou on our lips, O, Pride, when our hands were about to join?

CAMILLE. Who followed me? Who speaks beneath this vault? Is it you, Perdican?

PERDICAN. Blind fools that we are; we love each other. What were we dreaming, Camille? What vain words, what wretched follies passed between us like a pestilent wind? Which wished to deceive the other? Alas, this life is in itself so sad a dream; why should we confound it further with fancies of our own? Oh, my God, happiness is a pearl so rare in this ocean of a world. Thou, Heavenly Fisherman, hadst given it us; Thou hadst fetched it for us from the depths of the abyss, this priceless jewel; and we, like spoiled children that we are, made a plaything of it. The green path that led us toward each other sloped so gently, such flowery shrubs surrounded it, it merged in so calm a horizon and vanity, light talking, and anger must cast their shapeless rocks on this celestial way, which would have brought us to thee in a kiss. We must do wrong, for we are of mankind. O, blind fools! We love each other—!

CAMILLE. Yes, we love each other, Perdican. Let me feel it on your heart. The God who looks down on us will not be offended. It is by His will that I love you. He has known it these fifteen years.

PERDICAN. Dear one, you are mine.

(He kisses her. A great cry is heard from behind the altar.)

CAMILLE. It is my foster-sister's voice.

PERDICAN. How does she come here? I had left her on the staircase when you sent to bring me back. She must have followed me unobserved.

CAMILLE. Come out into the gallery; the cry was from there.

PERDICAN. What is this I feel? I think my hands are covered with blood.

CAMILLE. The poor child must have spied on us. She has fainted again. Come, let us bring her help. Alas! it is all cruel—

PERDICAN. No, truly, I will not go in. I feel a deadly chill that paralyzes me. Go you, Camille, and try to restore her.

(Exit Camille.)

PERDICAN. I beseech of you, my God, do not make me a murderer. You see what is happening. We are two senseless children. We played with life and death, but our hearts are pure. Do not kill Rosette, O, righteous God! I will find her a husband; I will repair my fault. She is young; she will be happy. Do not do that, O, God! You may yet bless four of your children.

(Enter Camille.)

PERDICAN. Well, Camille, what is it?
CAMILLE. She is dead. Farewell, Perdican!

(End of No Trifling with Love.)

Made in the USA
Middletown, DE
21 June 2021